The Section 8 SECRET

Written by:

Michael McLean - Section 8 Landlord
Mystery Writer - Section 8 Manager
Section 8 Tenants of Mike McLean

Copyright © 2009 by Michael McLean
All rights reserved.

ISBN: 978-1-0951-4989-8

CONTENTS

Introduction 1

Tip # 1: Section 8: What Is It And How Does It Work? 9

Tip # 2: How And Where Do I Apply? 13

Tip # 3: What To Say And What Not To Say
During My Interview 15

Tip # 4: Jurisdiction Jumping 25

Tip # 5: Transfer And Portability 31

Tip # 6: Politician Plot 33

Tip # 7: Bombardment! 39

Tip # 8: Persistence Pays 41

Tip # 9: Domestic Violence Victim 45

Tip # 10: Help For The Elderly (Part I) 49

Tip # 11: Help For The Elderly (Part Ii) 51

Tip # 12: If You Are A Veteran Or Know
A Veteran, You're In! 55

Tip # 13: Handicapped Help... 57

Tip # 14: Another Trick.. 59

Tip # 15: Pizza Packet 61

Tip #16: Shelter To Section 8 63

Tip # 17: Stay Reachable.. 71

Wrapping It Up! 73

INTRODUCTION

If you are looking to receive Section 8 Benefits, you have come to the right place! I know that for years you have been told, "The Section 8 waiting list is full" or "We're not accepting anymore applications." Well let me tell you what I also know, the waiting list is never full and they will accept your application! How do I know this? Well for the past thirteen years I have been a Section 8 Landlord and I have seen some amazing and creative ways that some of my tenants cut through the Section 8 red tape and were awarded their Section 8 Voucher. I would like to share all of these tips with you!

My name is Mike McLean and I am pleased to finally share some of the greatest tips ever with you. Most of these tips I received from my tenants but I also have a man on the inside. I have teamed with a very high up in Section 8 that has provided me with several tips that will place a Voucher in your hands very, very quickly. Tips that you are not suppose to know about. In fact, this entire book is the book Section 8 does not want ending up in your hands. Well guess what, it just did!

Everyday, people who are already receiving Section 8 assistance are terminated from the program or voluntarily re-enter the work field and give up their Voucher. Does Section 8 open up the waiting list when this happens? No. Do they call you and tell you to get down to the office immediately so they can issue you a Voucher? No. There **are** vacancies being filled every day but if you don't know how to put yourself in position to get that call, it's never gonna happen! There are so many ways to put yourself into this position, a position where you will either be handed a Voucher immediately or leapfrog everyone else on the waiting list. You need to be the person who gets the next call.

Here is how the Section 8 Voucher system works. When you apply for Section 8, the first thing they look at is your current living conditions and circumstances. They take into consideration your income, how many children you have, if you're receiving Social Security, etc, the list goes on and on. Then you are awarded points using the housing allocations points system. Your place on the waiting list depends on the number of points you have been awarded. The more points you receive, the higher up the waiting list you go. Now, that's where I come into the picture!

Let me let you in on a secret, 98% of the people applying for Section 8 are low income, have children, and need a better place to live, or they wouldn't be applying for Section 8. All 98% of you are in the same boat and that's exactly where Section 8 is going to keep you. It's the other 2% that get the help. These are the people who have figured out a loophole in the system that moves them ahead of everyone else. They

INTRODUCTION

have figured out a way to make it appear (if you want to say manipulate, that's fine) that they are in a much worse situation than you, dire straits if you will.

I would always wonder why I would rent a house to say a 45 year old woman and she would turn around and ask, "My daughter is also on Section 8, do you have any more homes available?" You and I both know how hard it is to obtain a Voucher so I knew it was not the "luck of the draw" that both mother and daughter each received a Voucher. No, there was more to it than that. Was there a secret that the mother passed on to the daughter on how to go about getting benefits? Was there a secret way to obtain a Voucher without having to play the waiting game? I was determined to find out how they did it so I simply started asking my tenants, "How did you get a Voucher?" You are going to be very, very surprised at their answers!

I'd say I asked over 400 of my tenants the same question and just about every single one of them did **not** do it the "legal" or "correct" way. You know the correct and legal way: calling and calling down to the Section 8 office, reapplying and reapplying, finally getting on the waiting list and sometimes waiting for years before the help you need finally arrives, if it arrives at all! Well, that's the correct and legal way and it doesn't work. You need help now, not six years from now!

Just about every tenant that I asked how they got onto the Section 8 Program had a different tip or story and guess what, they all worked! Some stories I thought were great and some I thought were absolutely crazy but they all indeed, worked. That's right, if I was asking them their story and they had the Voucher in their hands, what ever cocka- mamie story they used to get that Voucher, worked. I intend to tell you the top 17 tips to getting a Section 8 Voucher the quickest. These are the stories or scenarios that I think put a Voucher in my tenant's hands the easiest, quickest, and least painful.

Honestly, I don't know if the stories the tenants told their Section 8 Service Reps were completely true or not but who am I to judge? Will people lie or fabricate a story to get their family the help they need? You're damn right they will and who could blame them! Some of these people were ready to be put out in the streets but somehow they came up with a plan, got the wheels in motion, and found the help they needed. You can do the same with the tips in this book!

If one tip in this book does not work, move on to the next and keep plugging away. What I will tell you is that all of these tips **do** work and here is how I know they work. I would be rehabbing one of my homes and many neighbors would ask, "Is that home for rent?" I would answer "Yes, but I only rent to Section 8 tenants." Most would either reply, "That rules me out" or "How do I get on Section 8?" I would throw them some of the tips I gathered from my tenants and sometimes, even before I would finish completing the rehab, they would return with packet in hand and say, "Mike, I can't tell you how much I appreciate your advice, I received my Voucher and I want this house!" It got to the point where most of my tenants were on Section 8 and the person who made it happen for them was me. They started referring to me as "The Voucher Getter" and hence, that is where I came up with the idea of writing this book.

Nothing is easy in life and if you want something bad enough you've got to go out and get it. Many people can not work because they're single mothers, sick, or elderly. Now, you have got to do the next best thing which is go out and find help to put a roof over your family's head and food on the table. The person, who is told to get in line and wait with everybody else, probably will never get a Section 8 Voucher or the help their family needs. The person who takes a shot and orders this book stands a much greater chance of getting that help!

The tips in this book have worked for many others and I am positive that one of them will work for you. Some tenants were inventive, some were persistent, and some were just plain outrageous in their quest to receive a Section 8 Voucher and thanks to all of them and their tips, you will benefit greatly!

I also have another ace in the hole who you will greatly benefit from. Over the years of going down to the Section 8 office to sign leases and attend landlord meetings, I became good friends with one of the top Managers in the Section 8 system. I know a lot about how to get Section 8 benefits, but this guy knows much more than I do. I know many tenant scenarios and tricks but he knows legal loopholes that you can jump through and he has passed some really great ones on to me. All of which I will of course pass on to you.

Not only does my friend know legal ways that work, he knows what does **not** work. He informed me that there are certain things that applicants will say or do and this will disqualify them right on the spot. The applicant will not be informed they are disqualified but best believe they will not be brought back in for another interview or called when a Voucher becomes available. They don't know it but they have just taken themselves out of contention of landing a Voucher, just by opening up their mouths and saying the wrong things. My friend is going to make sure that this does not happen to you. He is going to go over what to say and what not to say in your interview. There are things that you can say and do that will make you outshine other prospective applicants and catapult you to the front of the waiting list.

Here is another thing that I want to tell you. This book is like no other because I don't just say, "go out and do this" or "go here and do that." No, I literally give you phone numbers and websites of where to go and what to do when you get there. I would have never known of these websites myself if I didn't have a guy on the inside who was willing to share this info with me. These numbers and websites are worth their weight in gold if you're trying to land a Section 8 Voucher. I have my guy on the inside and now you have you're guy on the inside, me!

INTRODUCTION

The last people that I have on the inside are my tenants. I informed some of them that I was writing a book on how to get Section 8 help and every single one of them thought it was a great idea. If I knew they had a great story, I had them write a paragraph or two on how they were entered into the program and if I liked the story, I used it in this book. You will be reading several of the top stories that I think would be most beneficial to you. The majority of my tenants don't like to share these tips so I had to offer them a hundred bucks if I used their story. Wow, even the tenants are entrepreneurs these days!

This entire book is only going to take you about an hour to read. It's short and sweet and gets right to the point. I could have put a lot of fat and filler in it to make it seem like more but that's the beauty of this book, there are probably 10,000 different ways people have tried to get on Section 8 and I'll bet 9,975 of them did not work. The tips in this book I know have worked. My tenants are the proof!

Believe me, you're gonna love this book. It's packed with true stories of people just like you who went the extra yard and succeeded in what they set out to do. Once you've finished this book, you'll pick out the tips you like best and immediately begin acting upon them and soon, you'll be a Section 8 Voucher holder! So without further ado, let's get started on getting you that voucher shall we. Here is tip # 1. . .

Tip # 1
SECTION 8: WHAT IS IT AND HOW DOES IT WORK?

I am going to keep this short and to the point because if you purchased this book, I'm almost positive that you know what Section 8 is. Section 8 (also known as the Housing Choice Voucher Program) is a type of Federal assistance provided by the United States Department of Housing and Urban Development (HUD), dedicated to sponsoring subsidized housing for low income families and individuals. It is more commonly referred to as Section 8, in reference to the portion of the U.S. Housing Act of 1937 under which the original subsidy program was authorized.

Federal housing assistance programs began during the Great Depression to address the country's housing crisis. In the 1960s and 70s, the federal government created subsidy programs to increase the production of low income housing and to help families pay their rent.

Housing authorities selected eligible families from their waiting list, placed them in housing from a master list of available units, and determined the rent that tenants would have to pay. The housing authority would then sign a lease with the private landlord and pay the difference between the tenant's rent and the market rate for the same size unit.

In essence, the way the Department of Housing wanted it to work out was the tenant would pay about 30% of their income for rent and the Federal Government would pay the rest, thus creating the Section 8 program. The Voucher Program was introduced in 1983. The reason most Voucher holders like the program is because it gives the Tenant the right to choose where they want to live. The reason the Government likes the Voucher program is because it saves them money on repairs (repairs to a private property are the responsibility of the landlord in most cases), and the reason Landlords like the Voucher program is that a certain portion of the rent is guaranteed, so the program really works for everyone involved.

Currently, the main Section 8 program involves the Voucher Program. A voucher may be either "project based" (where its use is limited to a specific apartment complex, Public Housing Agency) or "tenant based"(where the tenant is free to choose a unit in the private sector, is **not** limited to specific complexes, and may reside anywhere in the United States where PHA operates a Section 8 program.

Under the Voucher program, individuals or families with a Voucher find and lease a unit and pay a portion of the rent based on income, but generally no more than 30% of the family's income. Once the unit has passed inspection, the family is free to move in and hopefully live happily ever after!

Tip # 2
HOW AND WHERE DO I APPLY?

First of all, there are two different types of Housing assistance that you can apply for. The first is "conventional public housing" and the second is "housing choice" which are two separate programs requiring separate applications. The good news is that you can apply at the same office in most cases. You can contact your local Housing authority and they will tell you exactly where to go and what to bring with you.

To find your local housing authority or the housing authority that you are interested in using to help find you assistance, either look it up in the phone book under "government offices" which will be in the blue pages in the front of the phone book or let's say you live in Philadelphia, Google the word "Philadelphia Housing Authority" on the search bar and it will give you the main number to the Philadelphia Housing Authority. Once you have contacted the housing authority, you will tell them your situation and they will schedule you for an interview or "screening" to see if you qualify. You will let them know if you want "conventional housing" or "housing choice" assistance.

Conventional public housing is a term given to groups of buildings located at one site. Housing Choice is a program where applicants find apartments or houses owned by private landlords willing to rent under the program. PHA pays directly for part of the rent, based on federal regulations.

Your name will be placed on the waiting list based on the date and time of application. When your name appears at the top of the waiting list, the screening unit will review your application.

All applicants must successfully complete the screening process in order to be placed in a PHA unit. During the application process, you may check on the status of your application by calling a number that will be given to you by your Service Rep.

One thing to make note of, if you are trying to get into the "housing choice" program and apply for both programs, if you are accepted into the "conventional housing" and accept this assistance, you are no longer available for the "housing choice" program. It might be better to wait for "housing choice" rather than accepting the "conventional housing." It depends upon how desperate your situation is but "housing choice" does give you the freedom to choose your own home.

Tip # 3

WHAT TO SAY AND WHAT NOT TO SAY DURING MY INTERVIEW

After you apply for Section 8 Assistance, the first thing they will do is run a criminal backround check on you. If it comes back clear and they call you in for an interview, believe me, you're not done jumping through hoops! You still have another interview or "screening" if you will. Section 8 will call you and tell you a time and date to meet with a Section 8 manager or Service Rep. The things that they are going to tell you to bring with you are photo ID (drivers license preferred), birth certificate and social security card. Another thing they are going to want to see is some form or proof of income. It could be a paycheck, a W2 form, if you are receiving disability or social security, they will want to see your last pay stub.

If you don't have any income, you are in good shape but don't lie! I had a woman that I just finished signing a lease with and before her first month was even up, I received a termination notice from Section 8 informing me that my tenant had been terminated from the program. Because she was only on Section 8 for 15 days, I thought this had to be some kind of mix up. I called down to the Section 8 office to see what the problem was, there was no mistake!

I was informed that my tenant lied on her original application. She did not report the child support she was receiving from her four children. The child support was being automatically withdrawn out of her ex-husbands check. I don't know if this is how she got caught or if the ex-husband turned her in but whatever the case, she was terminated from the program and I was forced to evict her from my property.

In another case I had a woman that was a tenant of mine for nearly two years. This time I didn't receive a notice. Instead, I didn't receive my monthly rent check! Once again I called Section 8 and once again they didn't make a mistake. Turns out the woman was working full time for the water company and using her sister's name and social security number. Want to know how she got caught? When they ran the woman's social security number who was applying for Section 8, it showed she was employed. The woman swore up and down that she wasn't and when Section 8 finally got to the bottom of it, my tenant was arrested for welfare fraud. I don't know how she ever made out but I know she was terminated from the program and I would guess she had to pay back Section 8 all the money that she scammed from them.

It's a small world with big computers and when you start trying to hide taxable income and aliases, you're going to get caught; it's just a matter of time.

SECTION 8 INTERVIEW

There are things that you can get away with and I'll get to them later. One thing I'm not going to do is give you advice or tips that will land you in jail or have you kicked off the program as fast as you get on it.

Anyway, back to the interview. I'd like to tell you what goes on in the interview between tenants and Service Rep but I don't really know since I never sat in on one. Instead, I'm going to turn the reins over to my Section 8 manager buddy who has conducted and sat in on over a thousand of these things!
\

Thanks Mike and hello Section 8 hopefuls. First let me wish you well in your quest for finding housing for you and your family. It's not easy getting a Voucher but believe me, if you follow our advice, I truly believe you will indeed end up with a Voucher.

First things first, I know every single one of you have an entry plan. Whether it is a tip from this book or another strategy, everybody's goal is the same and that goal is to be handed a Section 8 Voucher. Now let me tell you this when it comes to your interview, your **exit plan** better be a hell of a lot better than your entry plan! Everybody who walks through those Section 8 doors is going to tell you why they want, need, and deserve a Section 8 Voucher. It is the people who tell you how they plan on getting off the Section 8 program that I would fight the hardest for.

They knew that at that very moment they were going through some really tough times in their life but they held their head high and had a plan on what they intended to do to get through these rough times and begin putting their life back together. I got so sick and tired of hearing the "woe is me" stories that I wanted to throw up. Do you want to know a few things of what not to say in your interview? Well here are some of the dumbest things that I was told by people trying to get assistance.

1. I once asked a woman during her interview why she deserved a Voucher more than anyone else that was applying. "Because I'm uneducated."
"Fine," I answered. "Why not go back to school?"
"I don't like school," she said.
"Well then you're always going to be uneducated," I returned.
"Don't you dare call me uneducated" she snapped.
"Uh, I didn't call you uneducated, you told me you were uneducated."
"Oh yeah, that's right, I forgot" she apologized.

2. I interviewed a woman who had three children, all over the age of ten. When I asked her why she was unemployable, she told me she didn't want to work. She wanted to be home with her children. I said, "Mrs. Doe, your children are in school all day." She said, "I know but when they are in school, it's the only chance I have to sleep." In other words, she didn't want to work so she could sleep all day. This is a person that if you put her into the program, she would never try to better herself and that is what the program is all about.

3. My third and final story comes from a single male, with no kids, who was built like a professional bodybuilder. In fact, that is exactly what he was striving to be. He had the nerve to tell me he couldn't work because he was in the gym for six hours a day and needed ten hours sleep per day to recover from his workouts. When I informed him that there was still eight hours left in his day, he told me that work would zap his strength that he was saving for the gym.

The common thread to these three stories is that these three people didn't get a Voucher. They didn't have any intentions on working or bettering their life. In fact, their greatest achievement in life would have been scoring a Section 8 Voucher. These are the types of people that myself or the Service Reps would never go to bat for. Their chances of receiving a voucher were slim to none.

What I wanted to see was a person with a little bit of pride and enthusiasm. Someone who walked in the office with their head held high, shook your hand and looked you right in the eye, and started giving answers not excuses. If I asked them why they couldn't get a job I wanted to hear, "I can and I intend to." If I asked what they intended to do while they were receiving Section 8 benefits I wanted to hear, "I want to get a part time job while I go to school to learn a trade or career." If I asked how long they thought this would take, I wanted to hear, "Every minute I'm not taking care of my children I will be working or working towards a degree." These are the people I wanted to help and felt good about helping, people who wanted to help themselves. Whether you walk into that interview and say that you are going to school to be a doctor or a maintenance man, both are better answers than excuses!

One woman even brought a schedule of her classes into the interview with her. She was going to school to be a nurse and in three years she would be graduating. I was very impressed with her and this is a tip that I highly recommend. If you are already in a school, bring something with you to prove that you are trying to earn a degree. Here are the top 10 things that you can do to really shine in your interview.

1. **Be on time**! I can't believe how many people were do in for a ten o'clock interview and didn't show up until after eleven o'clock. Right off the bat you're putting yourself in a hole. If the assistance that you *claim* you need is not worth being on time for, than that is exactly what the Service Rep will be thinking.

2. **Greet with a professional handshake.** Walk right into that room, introduce yourself, and stick your hand out for a shake **before** you sit down. Greet them with a firm (not bone crushing) handshake, three shakes is the number of pumps in a traditional handshake. Don't give it one of those handshake / over the shoulder hugs either. A professional handshake with your introduction is plenty.

3. **Relax!** Take a deep breath and relax. The person who is interviewing you knows that almost

everyone has some degree of nervousness during the process and will not think you are weird or hiding something if you're fearful. It's just a normal part of every interview.
4. **Don't mumble or slouch.** Speak clearly and don't slouch in your chair or lean back on it. It's good to be relaxed but you don't want the Service Rep to think you are a professional interviewer for Section 8 benefits.
5. **Dress well!** Even know you need help and are applying for assistance, dress well, it really makes a huge difference. A first impression goes a long way no matter what you are applying for.
6. **Be honest and don't ramble.** The more you ramble on about stuff, the more you put your foot in your mouth. "He who speaks much is much mistaken." A simple yes or no to some questions is fine and if you feel you have to elaborate, keep it short and sweet.
7. **Present your goals.** Present your goals and explain how long and when you plan to no longer need assistance. You **are** going to be asked this question so come up with some great answers and practice them.
8. **Don't complain!** Don't cry, complain, or make excuses about why you are in the predicament you are in. Also, don't beg or plead for help. The Service Rep knows why you are there and she knows you need help. It's your time to get her to like you and your career plans, not time to make her feel sorry for you. Crying for help will hurt,

not help you. One prospect said something in her interview that made her shine like a diamond. She said, "I want to be the victor, not the victim." I put a packet in her hand by the end of the week!

9. **It is okay to ask questions.** Hey, this is an interview and you want to know what's going on also so it is okay to ask some productive questions. "What's the next step", "How will I be notified?" "Are there any courses I can take that may speed my time on the waiting list?" are all good questions. "When do I get my Voucher?" "I don't have to work, do I?" and "How come my friend got a Voucher and I didn't?" are all questions you shouldn't ask. Also ask the Service Rep if the have any literature or brochures for schools in the area that offer students career training. It will plant that seed that you do want to help yourself.

10. **Thank your interviewer.** Thank your interviewer for their time, tell them to enjoy the rest of their day, shake their hand and get the hell out of there! I can not tell you how many people would get done their interview and then want to hang out it the office or the waiting room. Not only would they want to hang around, they would start bugging anybody and everybody with ridiculous questions. If someone was already on Section 8, they would ask them, "How long did it take you to get that Voucher?" If they heard I was the manager, they would ask me if I could pull some strings for them. If a landlord walked through the

door, they would ask him if he had any houses available, as if they already had the Voucher in the bag! Rather than be a pest, believe me, the best thing that you can do for yourself is give a hearty thank you and go home and wait for that call.

Tip # 4
JURISDICTION JUMPING

Okay, I'm gonna cut right to the chase and say what I have to say here. Most people, who need Section 8 assistance, live in the inner cities. When you live in the city, what do you get? Congestion, crowds, and overpopulation. What does that have to do with you? Well now instead of competing with say one thousand people for a voucher, you're sometimes competing against ten thousand people. Your chances of getting help become slimmer and slimmer! What can you do? Jump Jurisdictions!

Here is what I mean. Most of my tenants were applying for Section 8 in Philadelphia which only carries 15,000 vouchers for a city with the population of over one and a half million people. Meanwhile, if you take a half hour ride outside of Philadelphia to a surrounding suburb, some of the Housing Authorities don't even have a waiting list! You can apply, be processed and interview in the blink of an eye. Within weeks you could literally have a voucher in your hands and be on your way. Now, here are some tips.

Get on your computer and go to Google. Type in the search bar, highest income counties in the United

States – Wikipedia and click on this link. Scroll all the way to the bottom of the page where it says, "highest income counties and places by state." Now click on your state.

My state, which is Pennsylvania, gives me the richest county at #1 (Green Hills, Washington County at $124,279 average income) to the poorest county, #2,924 (Howe Twp. Forest County at $5,223 average income). Obviously, you want to find the "highest per capita income" that is closest to the city you wish to live in. The reason for this is very simple. If the "per capita income" is high, less people in this county need financial help or housing assistance. The poorer the county, the more people need help.

As an example, I'm going to do Philadelphia. If I were looking for help, I would either go to Montgomery County Housing Authority (about fifty minutes outside of Philadelphia) or Chester County Housing Authority (also about fifty minutes outside of Philadelphia). I see that there are several cities in these counties with high "per capita income".

My next step is to Google search "Montgomery County Housing Authority" and "Chester County Housing Authority." The first reason I'm searching them is to see if they exist. I want to make sure that these counties have a Housing Authority in place. Most do but some do not. After doing my search, I see that both counties do indeed offer Housing alternatives.

The next thing I look for is their address, **not** their phone number! You want to go there in person and apply, do not try to apply over the phone. Here is where my ace in the hole comes in handy again, you know, my Section 8 manager friend. He told me that if anybody just called out of the blue to see if Section 8 was accepting applications or if there was any room on the waiting list, the answer was always "No". If someone didn't take the initiative to come into the office and ask for information face to face, the answer they received was always going to be "No."

Now if someone came into the office with good manners and had a great attitude, sometimes even if Section 8 was not accepting applications, he or someone on his staff would make an exception and process this person. It's all about attitude and if you have a good one, it can make it a hell of a lot easier.

Another thing that he told me was that it is much easier to tell someone over the phone that there is no help available rather than telling them face to face. Do yourself a favor and go directly into the office. Even if they tell you that you have to schedule an appointment, you have already showed them some initiative on your behalf. Anyway, many of my tenants received their Voucher by Jurisdiction Jumping. Below is a brief story told by a tenant of mine.

I grew up in a small town in Pennsylvania. In the summers I would visit my family in Philadelphia. Those visits were the best times I've had in my life. I loved the hustle, the hip clothes and just the way everything was at your fingertips. At 22, I found myself a single parent with a low paying job. I still lived at home because I just couldn't afford to pay rent so I decided to start a new life and move to Philadelphia, where I knew I could move in with family.

*Not to burden my family members, I tried to put my names on their housing lists but I was told that one list was closed and another had a waiting list that was years long. Discouraged, I moved back home with my mom. After telling a neigh- bor of my short stay in Philadelphia, she told me that there was a local housing authority one town over. I never knew small towns offered housing assistance but the good news didn't end there. *

When I walked into the local housing authority and filled out a Section 8 application, I asked the secretary how long the waiting list was. She said, "Dear, there is no waiting list, we have housing Vouchers available immediately." Within a month I was called back for my intake Voucher interview. I was happy to get housing assistance so quickly but still dreamed of living in a major metropolitan city. When I spoke to the interviewer about my dream of living in the big city she says, "I have good news for you, we offer portability, which allows you to transfer your Voucher to any housing authority in the country." I was stunned and almost jumped for joy right in the interview booth.

I immediately asked her to transfer my Voucher to Philadelphia and she began the process of sending my paperwork to Philly. Within two months, I was a small town girl living in the big city with my rent paid for.

A. Winslow

Hey, two months isn't that bad. Throw in a couple of my tips with this one and you might be able to cut it down to four or five weeks!

Tip # 5
TRANSFER AND PORTABILITY

Now after reading tip # 3 you might be saying, "Hey Mike, I don't want to live with farmers out in Timbuktu," but here comes the good news. You can transfer your voucher to any Housing Authority in the country! It's called "portability" and it is offered by all Housing Authorities.

In some cases, as quick as you get your Voucher you can put in for a transfer without ever having to live for one day in Timbuktu. Soon as you get you're Voucher, put in for a transfer to where you want to go and it's done. The Service Rep will even help you fill out the transfer form and it's done, you'll be on your way.

Some Housing Authorities might require you stay for the duration of one lease term. Depending upon which Housing Authority accepts you will determine how long you have to stay with them. If the Housing Authority requires all leases to be a one year lease (most often the case), or if the Housing Authority requires you to sign a two year lease is how long you will be living in this county or city.

When the lease is three months from expiring, inform Section 8 and your landlord you will not be renewing the lease and fill out your transfer form, then, you will be aloud to move anywhere in the entire country! Hey, you might even get to like the house and town you have moved to and decide to stay. I've seen it happen.

Tip # 6
POLITICIAN PLOT

Sometimes it's not what you know, it's who you know. Right now if you are waiting to be accepted into the Section 8 Program, you definitely don't know the right people. Let me introduce you to them! The people you want on your side are your local and state representatives and here are a couple of ways you can find out who and where they are.

1. Get on your computer and go to Google. Type in your city followed by "state representatives." Mine would look like this, "Philadelphia State Representatives". You will be able to look up your state or local representative by zip code. The address and phone number of their office will also be available.
2. Go to your local court house or police station and ask for this information.
3. Go to your local post office and ask for this information. The post office is also a government office and someone there will be able to help you.
4. If there is a free Public Library, they are also funded by the government and they will also be able to point you in the right direction.

Okay, now you have figured out who they are and let me tell you what they can do for you. First of all, they can make life a whole lot easier for you! They can speed up your time on the waiting list by 100 miles per hour and I've seen it happen. Ya see, the entire Section 8 Program is funded by the Federal Government. Naturally these are the people that **you** put in charge so the pressure is on them to do the right thing by you if they want to stay in office. Are these people just going to call Section 8 and say hey, "Jane Doe just called me and said she needed help so get her a Voucher together?" Hell no, that's not going happen in a hundred years.

A Politician's request goes along way but they are not going to help you unless you help them. It's kind of like an, "I'll scratch your back if you scratch mine" deal. Here is how you're going to scratch their back so good they'll be demanding Section 8 to issue you a voucher!

1. If it is voting time, that is when they will need your help the most and it is a great time to strike. Not only will the State Rep need your help, he or she will be in and around the office a lot and so will you.

2. Offer to let him put a sign up on your front lawn. If you don't have a front lawn (which is probably why you purchased this book), volunteer to go around the neighborhood banging on doors and asking other people if the State Rep can plant a sign on their front lawn. The more signs you land, the more attention the State Rep will pay to

you. Make sure if you land ten signs in one day, you tell him that you landed ten signs. Don't let anyone take the credit for your hard work.
3. Volunteer to hand out and distribute fliers or brochures throughout the neighborhood. It's not a hard job and you can use the exercise.
4. Offer to work the phones in his office. I really like this one because instead of being outside doing things for the State Rep, you are on the inside and it is a good chance you are going to get some one on one time with him or her.
5. Offer to hand out fliers at the voting booth or do whatever you can on voting day.

There are so many things that you can do for a State Representative that I could go on forever. The important thing is to get out and offer your help. Believe me, if you are offering, they're not refusing. Anybody who is willing to help them out is another body and another vote in their quest to stay in office. When you get to know him or her a little is when you want to plant your story on them. Make it good and I'm sure they will help.

Below is how a tenant of mine was moved to the top of the waiting list, simply by going into the State Representatives office and asking for help. She skipped the volunteering part altogether so that just shows you the pull that some of these politicians have.

I was a mother of four and living in the projects. I was afraid to let my kids outside, scared to death that a stray bullet from the many drug dealers could hit them one day. My apartment was roach infested and badly in need of repairs. When I called my management office to complain about the conditions of my apartment it went on deaf ears. Five years earlier, I had applied for Section 8 at the local housing authority and always held out hope that I would be called to the top of the waiting list but that call never came. I was at my wits end and was considering leaving my apartment and just moving to a shelter. It might sound crazy but I thought the shelter might be safer.

I called my girlfriend who had a Section 8 Voucher and was living in a nice area of the city surrounded by homeowners. I asked her how long she waited until she got called in for her Voucher. She told me there was no wait for her. She went on to tell me the story how she was at a political rally for a local state representative, assisting in handing out fliers for her re-election campaign. She told the state representative her sob story about how she was a single mother living in a bad neighborhood and was struggling just to make ends meet. The state representative asked her if she was on any housing lists. My friend told her she had just applied for Section 8 but was told the list was closed. The state representative told her that she would make a couple phone calls to see if she could help her out.

A week later my girlfriend receives a letter in the mail saying she had reached the top of the Section 8 waiting list! Now, my girlfriend doesn't know for sure if that conversation with her state representative led to that letter but you can only assume so. So I looked up my local state representative in the phonebook and went to his office. I told the secretary in the office my situation and she walked back into the state representative's office. Two minutes later she comes back with a business card with a phone number written on the back. The secretary tells me to call the number and tell the person that they are a "personal friend" of the representative. Mind you, I still had not met the man but now I was a "personal friend."

The next day I call the number and tell the individual on the other line that I'm a "friend" of the representative and that I've been stuck on the Section 8 housing list for years. The individual, who never reveals her name, asks me for my personal information and says I should receive information in the mail in the next couple of weeks. To my amazement a month later I receive a letter that I too had reached the top of the waiting list.

I don't know how they did it or who they called but two state representatives helped my friend and I get Section 8 Vouchers. With our

Vouchers, we were able to find suitable housing for ourselves and our children in decent neighborhoods.

~ V. Johnson

I know I said her story would be short, sorry; it didn't work out that way. Anyway, you should get the point. Make these politicians work for you the way Mrs. Johnson made them work for her. They really do have a lot of pull; just make sure they are pulling the strings for you!

Tip # 7
BOMBARDMENT!

Everybody who went to school remembers the game bombardment. It was like dodgeball but instead of one ball, you had fifty of them being thrown at your head all at once! Well this is what you're going to do to your surrounding Housing Agencies. Let me explain.

Not a lot of people know this but you need not only apply at one Section 8 Housing Authority. You can and should apply at as many as you like. Most people who want to live in say, Philadelphia, will only apply for assistance at the Philadelphia Housing Authority office. Then they will sit back and hope they are lucky enough to get that call. Well I believe that you create your own luck in life. If the lottery is up to 100 million and you purchase one ticket but the guy behind you purchases a hundred tickets, the guy behind you has a much greater chance of hitting the lottery than you do. My point being, the more housing authorities that you apply at, the greater your chances become at being accepted into the program.

One of my tenants applied for assistance at eleven different Housing Authorities and received her

Section 8 Voucher from the Chester Housing Agency six months after applying there. After staying in her home for one year, she put in for and was granted a transfer. She has been a tenant of mine for the past four years. She told me that even after she was entered into the program via Chester Housing, she still received two more calls from other agencies that she had applied at.

The more irons you have in the fire the better your chances become so get out there and start applying! Here is my best tip on finding Housing Authorities that are near you. Go to Google and type the letters, "phada" on the search bar. It will bring you to a link that says, "Public Housing Authorities Directors Association". Don't click on the link. Just look under it and the third sentence will read, "Housing Authority Websites". This is the link you want to click on. It will give you your state and a ton of Housing Authority websites that you will be able to click on and see how near they are to you. If they are within an hour of you, I would strongly suggest jumping in your car and applying.

Tip # 8
PERSISTENCE PAYS

Okay, remember when I told you that some of the ways my tenants received their Section 8 Vouchers were outrageous? Well here is one of their stories.

I had a tenant with four kids who while waiting for assistance was living with her mother. She would call the Section 8 office about once a week to see if there was any availability or openings. Every time she received the same answer which was, "No." She had finally had enough of the phone abuse so she started visiting the Section 8 office, **every day!**

That's right. She would send her kids off to school and head directly to the Section 8 office where she would sit from 9 a.m. to 3 p.m., until she had to pick her kids up from school. The next morning, it would start all over again. From 9 o'clock till 3 o'clock, all day, every day for five months straight. She said they finally got tired of looking at her and issued her a voucher. The squeaky wheel gets the oil and in this case, her persistence really paid off. Below is her story.

THE SECTION 8 SECRET

Hello, my name is Dana Wright and I have been a tenant of Mister Mike's for five years now. Being a tenant is the easy part, getting help is the hard part so when Mike asked me to write a quick story on how I got on Section 8, I told him I would be glad to help if my story could help someone else so here goes.

I was 28 years old with four kids and had no place to live. The father of my four children had been incarcerated and this left me to fend for myself. The only choice I had was to move into my 65 year old mother's one bedroom apartment. With four kids and myself living there, I knew it was only a matter of time before my mom would have been sending us on are way.

I tried desperately to call Section 8 to see if there were any way they could move me up on the waiting list or find me an opening but it was always the same story. They continuously told me no and most of the time they were very rude and short on the phone with me. I didn't give them any attitude and I felt there was no need for them to be giving it to me so I finally went into the office and didn't leave for over four months. Day in and day out I sat on that chair reading a book and waiting. It beat being at my mom's house and being asked when I would be leaving, so the Section 8 office was more of a comfort spot for me.

I got to know all of the employees by first name and soon became friendly with most of them. To kill time, I would take out the trash for them, walk to the store if they needed anything, and would even run the vacuum in the waiting area. I am a very friendly person and have a great outlook on life and I knew that once they saw the true me and heard my story, they would get me and my children the help we so desperately needed.

They finally pulled a few strings and hooked me up with a four bedroom Voucher. I can't thank them enough and in fact, I still go down and visit them to this very day. My tip to you is stay strong and don't get down. If you look hard enough, help will find you! Good luck.

Tip # 9
DOMESTIC VIOLENCE VICTIM

Well here is another outrageous way a woman tenant of mine received a Voucher. This time the outrageousness was on the part of her ex-husband!

My tenant told me that she was being abused by her husband for years and had tried to get away from him numerous times. As with most battered women, she just could never make a clean break. She would have her husband arrested, he would stay in jail for a day or two and then return home and the entire scenario would soon repeat itself a day, a week, or a month later.

One of the reasons she could not make a clean break is because he worked and she did not. She stayed at home and took care of their six children. The only thing he was good for was keeping a roof over their heads and without him they would be out on the streets. Finally after a Christmas beating that put her in the hospital, she had had enough. It was either time to move out or be killed by this maniac, she chose moving! The problem was she didn't have anywhere to go. She went to apply for Section

8 assistance and when the women who waited on her saw her two black eyes she asked, "Are you the victim of Domestic Abuse?" My tenant, who I'll call "Doreen," answered yes and then as she said heard the best news she had heard in a very long time!

Since she was the victim of Domestic Abuse, she was processed and moved to the top of the waiting list as a "high priority case." She only had to wait four days before she was issued a Voucher. She and her kids moved out, she filed a restraining order against her husband, got a divorce, and things are going quite well for her.

She told me that Section 8 did a police check which showed nine incidents where the police were called to her old home and her husband was arrested. I'm sure this proof made Section 8 act as quickly as they did.

Look, I'm not condoning Domestic Violence in order to move to the top of the waiting list. I just thought I'd share this tip with any women who are afraid and are going through hell right now. There is a way to get out and one of your options should be Section 8.

I don't want to lead you down any wrong paths so I *really* checked into this with Section 8. It is true that you are moved up very quickly if you are a victim of Domestic Abuse but just like my tenant stated, "Section 8 wants proof of this Abuse." The best proof is going to be police reports and pictures of your injuries. All of which my tenant was smart enough to obtain and hold onto.

Of all of the routes to get on Section 8, I sincerely hope this is not the situation you are in but if it is, you now have an option thanks to Doreen!

Here are a couple more things that you may need to know. There are shelters set up specifically for Domestic Violence victims. The way to find them is to go your computer and enter in the search bar, "domestic violence shelters" followed by your state. I have also called a couple and the one in New York is very helpful. Even if you are not from New York and tell them that you are a victim, they will look up a shelter close to you and give you the shelter's phone number. The New York shelter's phone number is 1-800-621-HOPE. I was told by a woman case worker that you can only stay in a Domestic Violence Shelter for 90 days, then you will have to request a 75 day extension which in most cases, is always granted. Anyway, the entire time you are in the shelter, the workers there are going to be doing their best to get you into the Section 8 Voucher program.

Tip # 10
HELP FOR THE ELDERLY (PART I)

Another group of people who are accelerated through the Section 8 waiting list are the elderly. Section 8 knows that if you're poor and elderly, you desperately need help. A 65 year old man or woman can not pull themselves up from the boot straps and get a job as easily as a 30 year old.

Another reason the elderly need help so desperately is that their spouse, who may have had a pension or social security that was counted on, may have passed and now the other can not make it on their own. I am going to give out two tips that may not only help you but may also help someone who you know that is elderly and needs help. In fact in some cases, this tip can offer help for both of you at the same time!

Okay, first you have to know someone who is elderly that needs help, can qualify for Section 8 assistance and is related to you. One thing that I have to tell you about "related" and I'll get to that in a minute. Now what you want to do is simply apply for Section 8 assistance under their name and be part of their household. Now you along with the elderly person you're applying with will catapult right to the top of the list as a "high priority case", leaping over thousands of families who were not smart enough to apply under an elderly relative's name. This one really works like a champ and I know of several families who have received their Voucher in this fashion.

Now let me get to that "related" issue I was talking about. My Section 8 Manager friend informed me that Section 8 rarely, if ever, presses or investigates if the person you are applying with is really related to you. He said it was too much hassle and too much paperwork to investigate ancestors.

Here is the one thing that he told me you will need if you intend to apply this way. You will need some kind of proof that you and the elderly "relative" are living together and here is how you can get that proof! Before you apply for assistance, just have two pieces of mail with matching addresses and you are as good as gold. You can have a credit card bill, an automotive registration, a cell phone bill, or even a magazine subscription sent to your elderly relative's home or theirs to yours and this will do the trick. As long as you establish some type of paper trail that you are living together, Section 8 will accept it and you will get the Voucher you have been seeking.

Oh and one more thing before I put my final stamp of approval on this tip, **make sure** the elderly person is renting their home and does not own the home. Section 8 will not give rental help to a person or persons who are homeowners.

Tip # 11

HELP FOR THE ELDERLY (PART II)

The tip I just gave in part one was mostly for you (not the elderly). Now with this tip, I will gear it towards the elderly only. If you are elderly, Section 8 can indeed help you. Section 8 does not keep it a secret that one of their main objectives is to provide housing assistance for the elderly and if you're one of them, you have already got a leg up on thousands of others.

What I want to cover here in tip #11 is what you want to do with your Voucher once you get it. Ninety nine percent of the elderly who receive a voucher receive a one bedroom voucher with a small dollar amount provided for your rent. The more bedrooms attached to a packet, the bigger the dollar amount becomes. Here is an example:

A) A one bedroom Voucher will cover up to $600 in rent.

B) A two bedroom Voucher will cover up to $700 in rent.

C) And a three bedroom Voucher will cover up to $800 in rent.

Now number one, when you try to find a one bedroom house it's damn near impossible, they simply don't exist. Your next choice is an apartment but guess what, usually a one bedroom apartment is priced higher than the $600 in rent that your packet covers. Now where do you go? A retirement home!

That's right, if you are over 65 and have a Section 8 Voucher, a retirement home will most often accept it. I did not know this information either until I was informed of it by a cousin of mine who entered her mother into a retirement community. Below is her story.

I was forty five years old and my children had just graduated from college and had good jobs lined up. Finally my husband and I would have the empty nest we longed for. Without the financial burden of our children, we would be free to remodel the house, go on vacations on a moments notice, and finally plan for our retirement.

My parents lived about twenty minutes away, were in their seventies, and were enjoying their retirement. They had sold their house they lived in for fifty years and gave some of the money from the house to my children to help them through college. It was a decision that helped me and my children but it ultimately led to a situation that I never thought I would face.

HELP FOR THE ELDERLY (PART II)

My father suddenly became gravely ill. Within a week's time, he died of heart failure. This left my Mom all alone with only my father's social security check. All the money from the house was gone. My father was still working part time to help pay their rent at the retirement community. My mother was now stuck; she could not afford the rent alone. She had no choice but to leave the retirement community and move in with me. Just when I thought our house would be truly ours, my mother was moving in with me. Now I love my mother but it's not the same when you live together. Issues and fights arise at a moments notice.

I was talking to a friend over a cup of coffee, complaining of course about my mother moving in. She asks me, "Haven't you heard of Section 8?" I had never heard of it, she goes on to tell me that it's government rental assistance that will allow my mother to live on her own and they will pay her rent. I asked her immediately, "How do I sign my mother up?" She tells me how her mother went to an agency in the city that assisted the elderly with a variety of different services including housing. Her mother was recently widowed also and needed assistance with her rent. The agency did a referral with the local Section 8 office and within a month her mother received her Voucher. She was able to take her Voucher to a local retirement community who accepted Section 8 and within a month, was living in her own apartment rent free!

The next day I contacted the agency and they said all my mother had to do was bring her current income information and they would do the referral. Two weeks later, my mother got her own Voucher! I helped my mom look for a suitable apartment near my house and we found one only four blocks away. The landlord was more than willing to accept a Section 8 Voucher from a reliable elderly person like my Mom. I couldn't believe it, there was actually a program that could give me and my husband our home and our life back. Section 8 for the elderly, really was a blessing for us.

Tracey O'Donnell

Tip # 12

IF YOU ARE A VETERAN OR KNOW A VETERAN, YOU'RE IN!

One summer day I was working on one of my properties when I heard a knock on the door. When I answered, an older gentleman asked me if I was going to be selling or renting the property. I informed him that I would be renting the two bedroom property for $700 per month. He told me that the property would be perfect for him and his daughter but with his Army pension, the rent was to far out of his budget. I just bounced an idea off of him to check with Section 8 and see if they offered any assistance for Veterans and maybe they could help him. I gave him my number and told him to let me know how he made out.

Wouldn't you know it, within three weeks he gave me a call to see if the property was still available? He told me he was issued a two bedroom Voucher that would pay $604 of the rent. That left him paying me only $96 out of his pension check and he is still to this day a great tenant of mine. If that's all there was to this story, I wouldn't be telling it.

I know not everyone is a Veteran so let me tell you what's in this tip for you. First let me tell you what I learned from my manager friend. If you are a Veteran, you are moved to the top of the list. It's not a "high priority case", but you go above everyone else who is not a high priority case. Now here is the part of the tip that can help you even if you're not a Veteran. Remember in tip #11 when I told you that you could apply under an elderly person's household? Well you can do the same with a Veteran!

That's right, if you are "related" to or know a Veteran, apply under their name and be part of their household and you will hurdle over people and move up to the top of the waiting list.

Tip # 13
HANDICAPPED HELP

Once again, you don't have to be handicapped to take advantage of this opportunity. Handicapped people are considered "high priority" and are moved **very** quickly through the system. I'll keep this short and sweet because by now, I'm sure you know what you've got to do. You can't fake being handicapped but if you know someone who is handicapped, apply under their household and greatly improve your chances of getting a packet.

Another thing a lot of people don't know is that "handicapped" does just not mean wheelchair bound. There are many other handicaps out there and here are a few that someone you know or even yourself may have:

1. Respiratory System Problems (asthma, cystic fibrosis, sleep related breathing disorders) \
2. Heart issues (pacemaker, irregular heartbeat, heart disease)
3. Skin disorders
4. Mental disorders
5. Neurological disorders (epilepsy, Parkinson's disease, brain tumors)

6. Musculoskeletal System disorders (joint problems or bone fracture injuries)
7. Special Senses and Speech (blindness or any other visual impairment, deaf or other hearing impairments, speech issues)

The list of impairments goes on and on. Rule of thumb is if you can receive Social Security benefits for your impairment, you should be able to receive Section 8 for the same impairment as well. You'll also be glad to know that if you get denied your claim of disability, there are plenty of lawyers that will take your claim for free!

One more thing before I close out this chapter. If any of your children have disabilities of any kind, this will also increase your score and help your claim. So if your children are being treated by a doctor for any type of ailment, be sure to tell this to your Service Worker. Below is a chart of who is helped by Section 8 Housing.

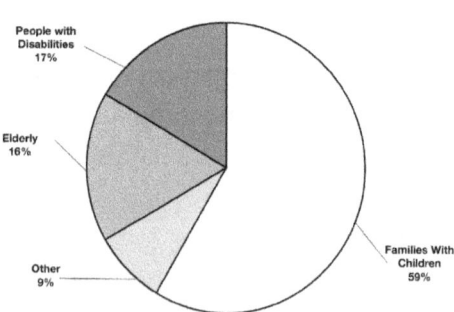

Who Is Helped by Housing Vouchers?

Tip # 14
ANOTHER TRICK

Okay, what do you do if the person you know who is handicapped, elderly, or a Veteran and already on Section 8 and living in a one or two bedroom unit by themselves? Move in with them! All they have to do is prove to their doctor that they need you at their residence for around the clock care. Once their doctor okays it, have the person you are staying with notify Section 8 and tell them that you are needed full time at their residence.

If the handicapped or elderly person is living in a 1-bedroom unit, Section 8 must then upgrade this person to a two bedroom unit. If you have children and are moving in with this person, Section 8 must also make room for your children. So let's say you have two boys and move in with a handicapped or elderly person. Section 8 must issue the handicapped or elderly person a three bedroom unit. One bedroom will be for you, one bedroom for your boys, and one bedroom for the elderly person that you are caring for.

I actually had this trick done to me in reverse. I had a one bedroom apartment that I just finished putting handicapped ramps in and within a year, my tenant informed me that she would be moving out. I asked her why and she told me that her niece had a child and was homeless. The only way her niece could get any assistance was to move in with her so that is what she did. The woman was upgraded to a three bedroom Voucher and lucky for me, I had a three bedroom house available. I built the necessary ramps, moved them in, and to this day they are all still tenants of mine.

Tip # 15
PIZZA PACKET

Here is another interesting story of how one of my tenants received her Section 8 Voucher. My tenant Myra was told that Philadelphia Section 8 was going to be opening up the waiting list. It was a Friday and while she was applying, a delivery from a local Pizza Shop showed up for the Section 8 office workers. She joked with her Service Rep that the pizza sure smelled good. The Service Reps response was, "It is good, we get two of them delivered every Friday."

Well a bell went off in Myra's head! She took the number of the Pizza Shop down off of the box and the next Friday, she purchased and delivered two pizzas to the Section 8 office herself. In fact, she started doing it every Friday. How long did this last you ask? Well, until she received her Voucher four months later.

If I'm doing the math correctly, that's about 18 weeks and 36 pizzas! If each pizza is ten bucks, this comes out to $360, not even half a month's rent. Her investment towards a Voucher paid off very well.

Look, I know that everyone is not going to get lucky enough to be in the Section 8 office when a pizza delivery comes strolling through the door but here is something that you can do. The next time you go down to the Section 8 office to check on your status, ask them if there is anyplace good to eat nearby. If they tell you, "Tony's Pizza" or "Just Wings," that means they have eaten there and they like the food. The next day, show up at the office with an order of it.

Are you ass kissing? Yes. Are you in some form or another, bribing them? Yes. But what you are also doing is getting yourself remembered! I'll bet the Service Reps forget 99% of the people's names who apply as quickly as they walk out of the door but with you it will be different. Show up with a couple of orders of food and soon you will be on a first name basis with these people and that is exactly where you want them. It is easier to deny someone assistance over the phone than it is to deny someone face to face who is also standing there with a pizza or two!

Tip #16
SHELTER TO SECTION 8

(This tip is written by the Section 8 Manager)

This one isn't for the faint of heart! Some people think they can just go and check themselves in a homeless shelter for a couple of days, get their Voucher, and live happily ever after, rent free. It's not that simple and if it were, the lines outside the shelters would be a mile long.

The first person you are going to have to get through at the shelter is the Housing Coordinator that will be assigned to you in intake. First they want to screen you and I mean *screen* you! You'll need everything that you need to apply for Section 8 (photo ID, social security card, proof of income, number of children and their information, etc.). You're also going to need references and here is where it gets a little tricky. The Coordinator will not only call your references to verify your story, they will also ask your references if they have room for you to stay as well. So before you check into the shelter, get your story ironed out with whomever you intend on using as a reference. Make sure they don't have any room at all for you.

The next thing is children. Let's say you have two children and when you check into the shelter, you tell you're Coordinator, "My children are staying at my parents' house," Well you just lost a lot of housing allocation points and you also lost a whole lot of credibility with you're Coordinator! Why? Because first of all, why would your parents take your children in and not you? Secondly, these Coordinators are not stupid and they know what you are up to. Let's face it, almost everybody knows about this tip but most don't know how to pull it off correctly.

You want and need that Coordinator to believe that you don't have anywhere else in the world to go except to that shelter. You want he or she to truly believe this is your last resort. What is the number one way to do this? Take your children with you!

I know it sounds horrible and you may think I'm nuts but it works. The reason you purchased this book is to get on Section 8 and I'm not going to start sugar coating things now. With your kids there with you, it also speed up the process. You'll jump ahead of everyone else who left their children with their aunt, or uncle, or whomever. Will it be tough bringing your kids to a homeless shelter? Of course! But it will be even harder trying to make it on the streets. Your children will survive and so will you. You will come out of that shelter much better off, with a Voucher in your hand to start finding a home.

Back to the Coordinator, when she checks you and your children in, she'll also have you fill out an application. The application is only to stay at the shelter, not for Section 8. Now, here is the bad news. You have to wait 42 days from the day you entered the shelter to apply for the Emergency Assistance Rehousing Program (EARP). If you are in the shelter for 90 days, you then can also apply for regular Section 8 assistance.

More often than not, if you follow everything that I just told you, you should get a Voucher in about six to eight weeks. Here is my last tip in this section. Sometimes you will get an offer from the Public Housing Agency (project based), before the Housing Choice Voucher Program. You have an option to accept or decline which ever agency makes you the first offer. If it is "project based," decline the offer. If it is for Section 8, gladly accept!

This is Mike again and I thought I would share a story of one of my tenants who stayed in a shelter while pregnant. She soon received her Voucher and has been a tenant of mine ever since. Her story may give you a little bit of an idea of what it is like in a homeless shelter.

I applied for Section 8 in Boston in 2005. At the time I had no children, was nineteen years old, and just starting my second year of college. I figured I would apply because things happen and you just never know if you are ever going to need help or not. Well, "you just never know" became a reality quicker then I ever imagined! At twenty one, I became pregnant while still living at school. I wasn't on the best terms with my parents so moving back in with them wasn't even an option. The dorms at my school did not allow children so I was forced to find alternative housing. The rents in Boston are the highest in the country next to New York and here I am, soon to be a single mom with school bills, books and now a rent payment in an expensive city.

My older sister who had a three year old son was on welfare and living with friends trying to figure out her next step. I didn't want to end up like my sister. I wanted to have this baby but still get my degree and make a life for myself. I heard through friends that if you enter the Shelter System, they will refer you to the emergency Section 8 assistance program. I was hesitant about entering a shelter but the timing was right. The current semester was coming to an end and summer vacation was right around the corner. I figured I could enter the shelter system and be in my new apartment by the fall semester. Well it certainly wasn't the summer vacation I was looking for but in the end, it was all worth it.

In Boston, to enter the shelter system, you have to go to the Emergency Assistance Unit in South Boston to be processed. It took me two attempts to actually go through with it. The first time I went, the scene was crazy! There were people stretched out in chairs everywhere, with kids looking like they hadn't slept in days. Others were yelling and cursing due to lack of service and just outright frustration. I decided at first that I couldn't go through with it and didn't want to be pregnant in a place such as this. About a week later as the semester was coming to an end, I realized that I had to make a decision for not only myself but also my baby.

The second time we went it wasn't as crazy. Yes there were still a lot of people waiting and waiting, but it was much calmer. It was May 15, 2006. You will always remember the date you went in not only because it was the day you went into the shelter system, but also because you will have to wait 42 days from the date you entered before you can apply for emergency Section 8. I was lucky because I had already applied for regular Section 8.

Upon my arrival I checked in and waited... for hours! Finally I was called by the intake worker who asked for identification and had me fill out an application. At the end of the application I had to explain why I was there, they really have to confirm that you have no place to go. Make sure before you enter the shelter, you have someone on the outside who can vouch for you. I used my sister as a reference and called her real quick before they got around to confirming my story. Then I went back to the waiting room, hoping my sister would play her part.

Again they called my name. "We were able to reach your sister but she refused to take you in." I later called my sister back to find out what she told them and let her know what stage of the waiting game I had reached. My sister played her part to a tee. She told them, "Hell know, she can't stay here" and ,"Don't call my house again". My sister is very dramatic and I'm sure that helped. I continued to wait.

Finally I was called again; they were ready to place me. I was sent to a tier 1 pregnant women's shelter in South Boston. My arrival at the tier 1 was pretty much the same as everyone who came before and everyone who came after; under the cover of night, hungry and tired as hell. When I arrived the staff gave me a briefing on the rules of the facility, a bagged lunch, toiletries, sheets and a blanket. They escorted me to my room, which was a cubicle in a room with about seven other cubicles. In the main area of the room were a sofa, two chairs, and a television. Each cubicle had a twin size bed, a nightstand, a chair and a wardrobe. There were two rooms on each floor; between the rooms was the shared bathroom (3 toilets, 3 sinks, a bathtub, and 3 shower stalls). I thank God that the place was kept pretty clean.

I entered my assigned room under the watchful eyes of the other women peeking out of their cubicles to size me up. My time in the maternity shelter went by slow, I continued to go to school in hopes that it would help speed things along as well as keep me focused. Most of us also spent our time preparing for our babies and planning for the future, praying that we would be out of the system and into our own homes before our babies were born or at least be placed in a tier two shelter. We called and called and called Section 8 to check the status of our applications.

I befriended some of the other woman, whom I sometimes affectionately refer to as "shelter buddies" on the rare occasion that I speak of my time in the shelter. It was easy to form bonds there. We were all pregnant and whatever our reasons, we were all there together trying to find a way. The women who bonded looked out for each other and we waited together.

In August, I was informed there was a spot available for me in a tier two family shelter in downtown Boston. The shelter made it a point to screen all of their potential clients not only to make sure that they would not be trouble but to make sure that they had goals and were prepared to take action to reach those goals. They had staff in place to assist in locating jobs, housing, childcare and schools. A day after finding out about my transfer, I found out my Section 8 assistance had finally been approved. I can't tell you how grateful I was to find out that I wouldn't be bringing my new baby, who was due in October, home to a shelter.

August was spent searching for a suitable apartment with my Voucher. I signed my lease a day before giving birth to my baby. When you apply to "wait" via the shelter system, you apply for both public housing (the projects) and Section 8 at the same time and you have an option to take whichever comes first. Whichever one you decide to take, you will be disqualified from receiving the other so be careful. Trust me, you want to wait for your Section 8 Voucher because you choose where you want to live. If you choose the projects, you can be sent anywhere. Not only did this whole experience make me stronger and more resilient, but it gave me a leg up when I needed it the most!

Shonda Pinkston

Tip # 17
STAY REACHABLE

All right, I have shared with you a bunch of tips on how to bypass or leapfrog everyone on the waiting list. The number one thing that you can do for yourself is stay reachable! If you want to keep yourself on the list and moving up, make sure that Section 8 can get a hold of you whenever they need to.

If you move, change your phone number, change your cell phone number or change your work number, be sure to notify Section 8 and tell them to make the change. Also, I would double check to see if they have it correct by calling down there from time to time. You can never be too careful.

I will guarantee you that if your name gets to the top of the waiting list and your phone is disconnected, Section 8 is going to move on to the next person who has their ducks in a row.

WRAPPING IT UP!

Well, that's gonna just about do it. I've told you everything I know, I've told you everything that my Section 8 manager friend knows, and I've told you everything that my tenants know. I think and know that these tips are the very best out there and I've seen every one of them work at least once!

Like I said in the beginning, Section 8 vacancies are being filled every single day. With the tips in this book, you will be the next to fill one of those vacancies. I sincerely wish you all the luck in the world and I hope you not only found this book useful, but I also hope you found it enjoyable. I put my heart into it, my friend put his ass on the line, and my tenants divulged some top shelf secrets and I hope that in some way, shape or form, you benefit from them. So keep your head up, hang in there, and stay motivated and persistent!

www.ingramcontent.com/pod-product-compliance
Lightning Source LLC
Chambersburg PA
CBHW070428180526
45158CB00017B/922